Examberry

Advanced Level Vocabulary
Book 4

So, **why learn vocabulary**?

The simplest answer is that as human beings, our most common means of communication is language. It is through the use of language that we express our ideas, needs and emotions. Words are the building blocks we use to share our intelligence. Having a greater number of words allows us to communicate with each other in ever more elaborate, sophisticated and persuasive ways.

On a more mundane level, expanding vocabulary is vital for children sitting 11+ grammar and independent school entrance exams. In both types of exam there is an element of creative or descriptive writing in which examiners are specifically looking for evidence of a well-developed vocabulary.

An extensive vocabulary suggests a child is well and widely read and able to put forward ideas and arguments in an intelligent way that will be helpful in all areas of academic life, not just in English language lessons.

The most natural way to increase a child's vocabulary is through reading a wide variety of books. That way a child can pick up new words while seeing them used in context. However, this involves years of enthusiastic reading and not all children are natural bookworms.

If your child is not a great lover of reading, this book will help expose them to new words and the exercises included with each vocabulary list will encourage your child to use these words, in context, in real sentences.

As they work through the list you can support your child's learning by encouraging them to use the newly acquired words in everyday speech, perhaps when describing their day, an incident at school, or a favourite film. As your child begins to use these previously unfamiliar words they will become more confident about using them in their work and their expressive writing skills will quickly develop.

Contents

Vocabulary 1

Learn the words below and then answer the questions that follow!

1. **Heritage** (n.): family history, tradition, culture, legacy.
   Cecile now lives in Britain, but she maintains her French **heritage** by celebrating French national holidays.

2. **Accumulate** (v.): to acquire an increasing number; to gather up, collect.
   If John continues saving money every month, he could **accumulate** a large fortune within a few years.

3. **Indestructible** (adj.): incapable of being destroyed; unbreakable, hardwearing.
   Plastic is **indestructible** and tiny particles can be found in all the oceans of the world.

4. **Keepsake** (n.): souvenir, memento, token.
   Carla's parents gave her a **keepsake** to remember them by when she went travelling.

5. **Grievous** (adj.): very severe, serious, grave, dreadful.
   Salvatore's injury was a **grievous** blow to the team's chances of winning the cup.

6. **Immoral** (adj.): unethical, bad, wrong, wicked, corrupt.
   The boy knew it was **immoral** to steal the buns but he was desperate with hunger.

7. **Advisory** (adj.): giving advice, counselling, consultative.
   Lisa was employed in an **advisory** role, because the company valued her knowledge and guidance.

8. **Comprehensive** (adj.): including all aspects of something; complete, thorough.
   Because he was the trip leader, Marcus had a **comprehensive** list of our parents' phone numbers.

9. **Possessive** (adj.): unwilling to share one's possessions; selfish, wanting attention, jealous.
   Matthew is incredibly **possessive** about his bicycle and refuses to lend it to anybody.

10. **Contradict** (v.): to dispute, deny, conflict with; to be the opposite of.
    When interviewed by the police, James immediately **contradicted** his brother's account of what happened during the robbery.

Exercise A: Synonyms

Write the word from the vocab list which is *most similar* in meaning next to each word listed below.

1. Severe _____

2. Tradition _____

3. Selfish _____

4. Unbreakable _____

5. Gain _____

6. Thorough _____

7. Souvenir _____

8. Deny _____

9. Consultative _____

10. Wicked _____

VOCAB 1 WORD BANK

Heritage

Accumulate

Indestructible

Keepsake

Grievous

Immoral

Advisory

Comprehensive

Possessive

Contradict

Exercise B: Complete the sentence

Write the most suitable word from the vocab list in the spaces below. You might need to change the form of the word; for instance, walk might become walked.

1. The children were being extremely _____ about their toys and refused to share them.

2. I was convinced that the table was _____ after Jim fell on it and it did not break.

3. Abdul had an _____ role at the school, to provide recommendations on how to improve teaching.

4. Our team won a _____ victory; we scored many goals and controlled the game.

5. None of the students dared to _____ the headmaster's stern lecture.

6. I bought my brother a _____ to remind him of me when he goes away to university.

7. Mum _____d enough air miles to pay for all our flights this summer.

8. Mila's family _____ is very intriguing, as her parents and grandparents all come from different countries.

9. Max's _____ injury caused much worry, but luckily his operation was a success.

10. Sean knew it was _____ to lie, even though it was to protect his friends.

Exercise C: Complete the sentence

Select the most suitable word from the choices provided.

1. I hope to _____ enough experience grooming my own dog to allow me to work at the poodle parlour.

    a. accumulate   **b. keepsake**   **c. indestructible**

2. Faris's project on rivers was not _____ enough, so unfortunately his grade was the lowest in the class.

    a. advisory   **b. possessive**   **c. comprehensive**

3. Maria's decision to lie in court, under oath, was both _____ and illegal.

    a. grievous   **b. immoral**   **c. contradiction**

4. I was not aware of Joe's Irish _____ until he explained that his parents had come from Dublin.

    a. heritage   **b. accumulate**   **c. indestructible**

5. Lydia is quite _____ about her closest friends, growing jealous if they spend time with other people.

    a. advisory   **b. possessive**   **c. comprehensive**

6. Mohammed lost his mother's precious _____ and she felt heartbroken.

    a. accumulate   **b. immoral**   **c. keepsake**

7. Alfie protested when he was given a detention but Miss Smith told him not to _____ her.

    a. possessive   **b. accumulate**   **c. contradict**

8. The superhero's rocket ship was made of a strong and _____ metal.

    a. heritage   **b. accumulate**   **c. indestructible**

9. The expensive war had _____ implications for the country's finances.

    a. grievous   **b. immoral**   **c. contradiction**

10. The maths test was only _____, to help our teachers put us in sets for next term.

    a. possessive   **b. advisory**   **c. comprehensive**

Vocabulary 2

Learn the words below and then answer the questions that follow!

1. **Moderation** (n.): self-restraint, self-control; reduction, weakening.
   I try to eat sweet things in **moderation**, ever since the dentist gave me a filling.

2. **Immeasurable** (adj.): vast, huge, extensive, incalculable.
   The treatment brought about an **immeasurable** improvement in Asha's condition.

3. **Enthusiastic** (adj.): showing enjoyment and interest; eager, keen, passionate.
   Despite having never played baseball before, Hamza was **enthusiastic** and ready for the challenge.

4. **Negotiate** (v.): to discuss, arrange, reach agreement on.
   The football star managed to **negotiate** a huge pay rise, after many meetings with the club management.

5. **Partially** (adv.): partly, to a limited extent, moderately.
   The whole family suffered from food poisoning after eating **partially** cooked chicken.

6. **Deceive** (v.): to mislead, swindle, cheat, fool.
   Nima's constant lies were intended to **deceive** me, but I saw through them.

7. **Pedestal** (n.): plinth on which a statue is placed; a position from which someone is admired.
   The statue could be seen clearly from a distance, on its tall **pedestal**.

8. **Characterise** (v.): to portray, describe, distinguish, define.
   The teacher liked to **characterise** Freddie as the class comedian, as he always entertained us with his jokes.

9. **Implausible** (adj.): hard to believe, unconvincing.
   The children enjoyed the special effects of the new superhero film, but the plot was **implausible**.

10. **Obstinate** (adj.): stubborn, unyielding, unbending, headstrong.
    The **obstinate** prime minister refused to give in to the people's demands after weeks of protest.

Exercise A: Synonyms

Write the word from the vocab list which is *most similar* in meaning next to each word listed below.

VOCAB 2 WORD BANK

Moderation

Immeasurable

Enthusiastic

Negotiate

Partially

Deceive

Pedestal

Characterise

Implausible

Obstinate

1. Partly _____

2. Mislead _____

3. Plinth _____

4. Stubborn _____

5. Broker _____

6. Define _____

7. Restraint _____

8. Unbelievable_____

9. Incalculable_____

10. Keen _____

Exercise B: Complete the sentence

Write the most suitable word from the vocab list in the spaces below. You might need to change the form of the word; for instance, walk might become walked.

1. John adored his mother; you could say that he placed her on a _____.

2. Daisy's explanation of where she had been all day was highly _____ and Mum did not believe her.

3. The complex film was difficult to _____, but critics settled on calling it a dark comedy.

4. Tina was _____ and refused to leave the concert until the last song was over.

5. I was not _____ when Dad said we had to revise for exams over the holidays.

6. One of the witnesses at the trial attempted to _____ the jury with his lies.

7. The ancient cathedral was _____ destroyed by fire, however, its beautiful tiled floor was undamaged.

8. The influence of Shakespeare on English language and literature is _____.

9. The city leaders refused to _____ with the terrorists and would not give in to their demands.

10. My grandfather attributes long life and health to _____ in everything.

Exercise C: Complete the sentence

Select the most suitable word from the choices provided.

1. No one could comprehend Lily's _____ suffering after her dog died suddenly.

   a. enthusiastic   **b. negotiate**   **c. immeasurable**

2. Dry, warm weather and strong winds _____ the climate of this region.

   a. obstinate   **b. implausible**   **c. characterise**

3. The concert hall made special arrangements for blind and _____ sighted visitors.

   a. partially   **b. deceive**   **c. pedestal**

4. The tight, uphill corner was difficult for the old car to _____.

   a. moderation   **b. negotiate**   **c. immeasurable**

5. The teacher did not believe Carl's _____ story about his lost homework and gave him a detention.

   a. implausible   **b. obstinate**   **c. characterise**

6. Mark was incredibly _____ and refused to go to bed when Dad told him to.

   a. deceive   **b. partially**   **c. obstinate**

7. Stacy is only allowed to play computer games in _____, because too much screen-time is unhealthy for children.

   a. pedestal   **b. moderation**   **c. immeasurable**

8. The conman tried to _____ the police by producing a fake passport.

   a. deceive   **b. obstinate**   **c. characterise**

9. James is an _____ hiker who encourages all his friends to go outdoors.

   a. partially   **b. implausible**   **c. enthusiastic**

10. The valuable vase was displayed on a golden _____ in the museum.

   a. negotiate   **b. pedestal**   **c. moderation**

Vocabulary 3

Learn the words below and then answer the questions that follow!

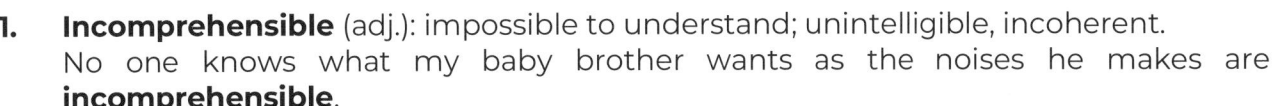

1. **Incomprehensible** (adj.): impossible to understand; unintelligible, incoherent.
   No one knows what my baby brother wants as the noises he makes are **incomprehensible**.

2. **Illicit** (adj.): illegal, unlawful, forbidden.
   Sadly, there is still an **illicit** trade in animal skins and ivory, despite efforts to catch the smugglers.

3. **Overdose** (n.): a dangerously high dose of a drug; excess, binge.
   The vet said we must be careful not to give our kitten an **overdose** of medicine, since the side-effects were harmful.

4. **Hereditary** (adj.): passed down at birth; inherited, genetic, inborn.
   Every member of the Frock family is extremely thin, and some say this is **hereditary**.

5. **Terminus** (n.): finishing point; often a transport terminal or last stop.
   Ealing Broadway is the **terminus** for the westbound Central and District tube lines.

6. **Liable** (adj.): likely to do something; prone, susceptible.
   After his ankle injury, Lawrence decided not to go skiing, as he was **liable** to fall over.

7. **Invariably** (adv.): usually, repeatedly, regularly.
   On Friday, we **invariably** have fish and chips for lunch at school.

8. **Mesmerise** (v.): to captivate, transfix, fascinate.
   The narrator's calm voice began to **mesmerise** the class; the children all sat still and listened intently.

9. **Self-defence** (n.): defending oneself through physical force; self-protection.
   Jake learned to protect himself from attackers, at a class in **self-defence**.

10. **Stimulant** (n.): energiser, reviver, boost, impetus.
    The government's new tax policy acted as a **stimulant** for smaller businesses to grow.

Exercise A: Synonyms

Write the word from the vocab list which is *most similar* in meaning next to each word listed below.

VOCAB 3 WORD BANK

Incomprehensible

Illicit

Overdose

Hereditary

Terminus

Liable

Invariably

Mesmerise

Self-defence

Stimulant

1. Illegal _____

2. Inclined _____

3. Boost _____

4. Captivate _____

5. Unintelligible_____

6. Excess _____

7. Finish _____

8. Self-protection_____

9. Usually _____

10. Inherited _____

Exercise B: Complete the sentence

Write the most suitable word from the vocab list in the spaces below. You might need to change the form of the word; for instance, walk might become walked.

1. Victoria is the best-known bus _____ in London.

2. When the mugger grabbed her bag, Jane used her karate moves in _____.

3. It is possible to take an _____ of paracetamol, even though it is not a very potent drug.

4. My grandad has a terrible sense of direction and is always _____ to get lost.

5. The doctors said that fortunately the lung disorder was not _____ and could not be passed down from parent to child.

6. The dishonest athletes used a chemical _____ to enhance their performance.

7. Dad hates commuting to work because the trains are _____ late in the morning.

8. The breathtaking feats of the circus acrobats seemed to _____ the audience.

9. Jim was so far away that even though he shouted, his words were _____.

10. The gangsters dealt in the _____ sale of forged and stolen passports.

Exercise C: Complete the sentence

Select the most suitable word from the choices provided.

1. Louise is _____ to be upset when she discovers that she failed the test.

   a. invariably   **b. liable**   **c. terminus**

2. The spy set up an _____ meeting with the double agent.

   a. illicit   **b. overdose**   **c. hereditary**

3. The magician began to _____ the audience with his clever tricks.

   a. mesmerise   **b. stimulant**   **c. self-defence**

4. The muffled station announcement about platform changes was _____ to most travellers.

   a. liable   **b. invariably**   **c. incomprehensible**

5. Many geneticists believe that traits such as height and intelligence are _____.

   a. overdose   **b. hereditary**   **c. terminus**

6. The court ruled that Carlos had acted in _____ and should not be punished for breaking his assailant's nose.

   a. stimulant   **b. illicit**   **c. self-defence**

7. Mum despairs because my sister _____ loses her school jumper by the end of term.

   a. invariably   **b. liable**   **c. incomprehensible**

8. I always call my mother ten minutes before arriving at the bus _____ so that she can pick me up.

   a. hereditary   **b. mesmerise**   **c. terminus**

9. The bodybuilder used a _____ so that his muscles would repair rapidly.

   a. illicit   **b. stimulant**   **c. self- defence**

10. At his birthday party, my little brother had an _____ of sweets and fizzy drinks, and became very excited.

    a. overdose   **b. hereditary**   **c. liable**

Vocabulary 4

Learn the words below and then answer the questions that follow!

1. **Morose** (adj.): sullen, miserable, downcast, gloomy.
   Teddy looked **morose** after he was reprimanded by the teacher.

2. **Zealous** (adj.): enthusiastic, passionate; showing keen support for a cause.
   Ursula converted to Buddhism and was devoted and **zealous** in her faith.

3. **Arbitrary** (adj.): random, inconsistent, haphazard, chance.
   The sports teacher's choice of players for the netball team seemed **arbitrary**, because some talented girls had been left out.

4. **Illogical** (adj.): unreasonable, irrational, unfounded.
   Denise's fear of being bitten by a shark in Cornwall was **illogical** but it spoilt the family beach holiday.

5. **Palpable** (adj.): obvious, intense, perceptible, noticeable.
   The tension in the room was **palpable** after England progressed to a penalty shoot-out.

6. **Irreparable** (adj.): impossible to repair, irrecoverable, broken.
   Arnold promised to compensate me after he caused **irreparable** damage to my laptop and I had to buy a new one.

7. **Insatiable** (adj.): impossible to satisfy, uncontrollable, greedy.
   Cyrus has an **insatiable** appetite; he could eat all day long.

8. **Manoeuvre** (v.): to move skilfully, navigate, negotiate.
   Lisa had to **manoeuvre** her bike carefully between the two cars to avoid a crash.

9. **Inseparable** (n.): unable to be separated; indivisible, bound together.
   Harry and Luca are **inseparable**; they are always together and are the closest of friends.

10. **Profession** (n.): job or career requiring a high level of training.
    After Franco had travelled the world and witnessed poverty, he decided on his **profession** as a doctor.

Exercise A: Synonyms

Write the word from the vocab list which is *most similar* in meaning next to each word listed below.

1. Irrecoverable_____

2. Irrational _____

3. Occupation_____

4. Greedy _____

5. Navigate _____

6. Perceptible_____

7. Sullen _____

8. Random _____

9. Enthusiastic_____

10. Indivisible _____

VOCAB 4 WORD BANK

Morose

Zealous

Arbitrary

Illogical

Palpable

Irreparable

Insatiable

Manoeuvre

Inseparable

Profession

Exercise B: Complete the sentence

Write the most suitable word from the vocab list in the spaces below. You might need to change the form of the word; for instance, walk might become walked.

1. Michael's demands for pocket money were _____; whatever he was given was never enough.

2. It was difficult to _____ around the tight corner, but Mum managed it by driving slowly.

3. The twins were _____, and would cry whenever they were split up.

4. Dad's choice of hotel seemed _____ because he didn't even check if it had a pool or restaurant.

5. Leila had an _____ fear of moths, as they had never done her any harm.

6. There was a _____ sense of excitement in the air as we approached the circus tent.

7. Sadiq felt _____ after his parents took the Xbox away.

8. Tim entered the _____ of journalism by writing for his local newspaper.

9. The bitter argument caused _____ damage to Lisa and Amy's friendship.

10. All around the football stadium, there were _____ fans, chanting.

Exercise C: Complete the sentence

Select the most suitable word from the choices provided.

1. Tina was unsure which _____ she would enter after finishing university.

   a. manoeuvre   **b. profession**   **c. inseparable**

2. Since she retired, Granny has become a _____ charity worker and is busier than ever.

   a. morose   **b. arbitrary**   **c. zealous**

3. The tension was _____ as the children lined up outside the exam hall.

   a. palpable   **b. irreparable**   **c. illogical**

4. Alex has an _____ hunger for success and devotes himself to studying hard.

   a. insatiable   **b. profession**   **c. inseparable**

5. Elyse tried to _____ herself out of working at the weekend but did not have a good enough excuse.

   a. zealous   **b. morose**   **c. manoeuvre**

6. Marco did not know what outcome he preferred for the election, so his vote felt rather _____.

   a. palpable   **b. arbitrary**   **c. illogical**

7. Salvaging the trade deal was impossible given the _____ relations between the two nations.

   a. irreparable   **b. inseparable**   **c. profession**

8. Everyone felt _____ about having to leave the beautiful holiday home.

   a. morose   **b. zealous**   **c. palpable**

9. It would be _____ to assume that Kit would win the race, since he was most unfit.

   a. arbitrary   **b. manoeuvre**   **c. illogical**

10. Pete and his new dog are _____, and spend every waking moment together.

   a. inseparable   **b. zealous**   **c. profession**

Vocabulary 5

Learn the words below and then answer the questions that follow!

1. **Invalid** (adj.): false, untrue, inaccurate
   James found evidence which proved Luka's scientific theory **invalid**.

2. **Reproduction** (n.): copy, duplicate; having children, breeding.
   There was a scandal when the gallery discovered that the painting was not a genuine masterpiece but a **reproduction**.

3. **Alienate** (v.): to make someone feel isolated; to estrange, ostracise.
   The class bully tried to **alienate** Jaiden by leaving him out of playground games.

4. **Sequential** (adj.): following a logical order; chronological, continual.
   The instructions set out a series of **sequential** steps for assembling the flat-packed table.

5. **Insignificant** (adj.): irrelevant, unimportant, trivial, worthless.
   Daniel's missed penalty was **insignificant** as we still won the match by ten goals.

6. **Mentality** (n.): way of thinking, mindset, attitude.
   I had a positive **mentality** at the start of the year, but I am less optimistic now after losing my job.

7. **Supple** (adj.): moving with ease, flexible, pliable.
   Niall's **supple** physique enabled him to perfect his gymnastics routine.

8. **Affirmative** (adj.): agreeing, positive, approving.
   The head teacher gave an **affirmative** response, agreeing with my proposal to improve the school's garden.

9. **Orchestrate** (v.): to arrange a piece of music so that it can be played by an orchestra; to arrange, fix.
   Mum managed to **orchestrate** her business trip so that she could visit her brother in New York.

10. **Simultaneous** (adj.): occurring at the same time; concurrent, coinciding.
    A team of **simultaneous** translators work at the UN to facilitate international meetings.

Exercise A: Synonyms

Write the word from the vocab list which is *most similar* in meaning next to each word listed below.

1. Attitude _____

2. Concurrent _____

3. Approving _____

4. Untrue _____

5. Duplication _____

6. Arrange _____

7. Chronological _____

8. Unimportant _____

9. Flexible _____

10. Ostracise _____

> **VOCAB 5 WORD BANK**
>
> Invalid
>
> Reproduction
>
> Alienate
>
> Sequential
>
> Insignificant
>
> Mentality
>
> Supple
>
> Affirmative
>
> Orchestrate
>
> Simultaneous

Exercise B: Complete the sentence

Write the most suitable word from the vocab list in the spaces below. You might need to change the form of the word; for instance, walk might become walked.

1. The famous musician was asked to _____ his new work for the Royal Ballet.

2. An _____ response from Mum about the party invitation seemed unlikely, as I was still grounded.

3. Our team's negative _____ meant that we were surprised to win any games!

4. Lola managed to _____ her classmates with her bad temper, including her best friends.

5. The fans all let out a _____ scream of delight when the singer appeared on stage at the festival.

6. The stain on my t-shirt was so _____ that no one even noticed it.

7. There was a _____ showing of the six Star Wars movies at my local cinema.

8. The ballerina was astonishingly _____ due to many years of constant exercise and training.

9. Mum's insurance claim was declared _____ because she had forgotten to submit it on time.

10. Zoologists study animal _____ in order to save endangered species.

Exercise C: Complete the sentence

Select the most suitable word from the choices provided.

1. The politician hoped his ideas would receive _____ votes in the House of Commons.

    a. supple   **b. affirmative**   **c. orchestrate**

2. My dad is a skilled artist and made a near-perfect _____ of Van Gogh's 'Sunflowers'.

    a. invalid   **b. alienate**   **c. reproduction**

3. Many athletes have a resilient _____ which helps them to overcome obstacles.

    a. mentality   **b. insignificant**   **c. sequential**

4. The news bulletin reported three _____ demonstrations taking place across the city.

    a. supple   **b. affirmative**   **c. simultaneous**

5. My uncle has managed to _____ the rest of the family with his spiteful behaviour.

    a. alienate   **b. orchestrate**   **c. reproduction**

6. The rider applied special polish to the expensive saddle to keep it _____ and smooth.

    a. invalid   **b. supple**   **c. mentality**

7. Dexter's contribution to the experiment was _____ because most of the data was gathered without his help.

    a. sequential   **b. insignificant**   **c. simultaneous**

8. Mr Jones said it was hard to _____ a huge cast of characters in the school play.

    a. affirmative   **b. alienate**   **c. orchestrate**

9. Tomas made an error on the job application form which caused the whole document to become _____.

    a. mentality   **b. supple**   **c. invalid**

10. The chess player thought of a _____ strategy that would lead her to victory.

    a. sequential   **b. alienate**   **c. reproduction**

Vocabulary 6

Learn the words below and then answer the questions that follow!

1. **Elude** (v.): to escape, avoid, evade, dodge.
    The robber tried to **elude** the security guards by sneaking through a back door.

2. **Treachery** (n.): betrayal of trust; disloyalty, infidelity.
    The double agent was sentenced to life in prison for his **treachery**.

3. **Meagre** (adj.): lacking in quantity; inadequate, stingy, sparse.
    The restaurant serves great food but in **meagre** quantities: all the reviews mention the tiny portions.

4. **Aversion** (n.): strong dislike, disinclination; hatred, loathing.
    I have an **aversion** to cats and cannot bear them to come near me.

5. **Condensation** (n.): water which collects on a surface; process of gas turning into a liquid.
    Condensation appeared on the front window of the car after Mum put the heater on.

6. **Existential** (adj.): relating to existence; about life and death; related to philosophy.
    David Attenborough argues that humans are an **existential** threat to many animal species.

7. **Defamation** (n.): damaging someone's reputation; slander, libel, abuse.
    The newspaper was sued for **defamation** after it spread a false story about the actor.

8. **Abstain** (v.): to refrain, renounce, stop, desist.
    My parents have decided to **abstain** from drinking alcohol during January.

9. **Appraise** (v.): to assess the value or quality of something; to evaluate, judge.
    The Chief Executive instructed his managers to **appraise** the work of junior staff and give everyone some feedback.

10. **Loiter** (v.): to wait around, linger, dawdle.
    The teacher told the students not to **loiter** in the corridor but to go and wait in their form rooms.

Exercise A: Synonyms

Write the word from the vocab list which is *most similar* in meaning next to each word listed below.

Elude

Treachery

Meagre

Aversion

Condensation

Existential

Defamation

Abstain

Appraise

Loiter

1. Inadequate _____

2. Slander _____

3. Evaluate _____

4. Linger _____

5. Evade _____

6. Living _____

7. Refrain _____

8. Hatred _____

9. Water _____

10. Betrayal _____

Exercise B: Complete the sentence

Write the most suitable word from the vocab list in the spaces below. You might need to change the form of the word; for instance, walk might become walked.

1. After I had a shower, the mirrors were misty with _____.

2. David was bored after the lesson so he chose to _____ in the playground.

3. Mary wondered if animals thought about _____ questions in the same way as humans.

4. I tried to _____ from chocolate after my dentist warned me that my teeth would rot if I ate too much sugar.

5. I could not believe Tommy's _____, after discovering that he had told the whole class our secrets.

6. Some Arsenal fans have an _____ to Tottenham players, because the teams are are rivals.

7. Dad was trying to lose weight and stuck to a _____ diet of raw vegetables.

8. Our escaped hamster managed to _____ us for several hours before we found him under the sofa.

9. At Parents' Evening, my teachers will try to _____ my performance this term.

10. The shocking claims made about the politician's personal life were false; they were simply _____.

Exercise C: Complete the sentence

Select the most suitable word from the choices provided.

1. Philosophy attempts to answer _____ questions, such as what happens when people die.

   a. existential   **b. defamation**   **c. abstain**

2. The cloud emerged due to the _____ of water vapour in the air.

   a. meagre   **b. aversion**   **c. condensation**

3. Mum asked a jeweller to _____ the value of her necklace, and sadly she was told it was worthless.

   a. appraise   **b. elude**   **c. treachery**

4. Dad asked me to come straight home after school and not to _____ about.

   a. defamation   **b. loiter**   **c. existential**

5. Giacomo has an _____ to bright light, so he must wear special sunglasses outdoors.

   a. abstain   **b. aversion**   **c. condensation**

6. The athlete prepared for the World Championships for months, but success continued to _____ her.

   a. elude   **b. meagre**   **c. appraise**

7. The pirate captain was baffled by the _____ of his crew, who tried to throw him overboard.

   a. defamation   **b. existential**   **c. treachery**

8. New government policies encourage young people to _____ from smoking.

   a. aversion   **b. abstain**   **c. condensation**

9. Many employees complained about the _____ salary, and demanded a wage rise.

   a. meagre   **b. appraise**   **c. elude**

10. The celebrity won his _____ lawsuit after the false news story was published.

    a. existential   **b. treachery**   **c. defamation**

Vocabulary 7

Learn the words below and then answer the questions that follow!

1. **Innate** (adj.): natural, inborn, inherent.
    Alexis has an **innate** talent for sports and exercise; he is a true athlete.

2. **Conscience** (n.): a sense of right and wrong; morality, inner voice.
    My **conscience** made me feel guilty after I took the last piece of cake.

3. **Utility** (n.): usefulness, value, benefit, practicality.
    The hikers appreciated the **utility** of their comfortable boots after completing the trek without blisters.

4. **Incoherent** (adj.): incomprehensible, unclear, confused.
    Nick gave us confusing and **incoherent** directions to the cinema, so we all became lost.

5. **Fretful** (adj.): distressed, miserable, unsettled, agitated.
    Ellie felt **fretful** when her cat disappeared; she barely slept until Fluffy returned.

6. **Indispensable** (adj.): necessary, essential, vital.
    Elodie was an **indispensable** member of the football team, as she scored most of the goals.

7. **Foreseeable** (adj.): predictable, expected, likely, anticipated.
    The meteorologist stated that it would continue snowing for the **foreseeable** future.

8. **Overtone** (adj.): additional effect or meaning; connotation.
    The head teacher's speech was factual but there was an **overtone** of anger as she described the damage to the library.

9. **Coincide** (v.): to occur at the same time; to correspond with.
    The opening of the exhibition has been planned to **coincide** with the film premiere.

10. **Excavate** (v.): to dig, unearth, uncover.
    The archaeologists managed to **excavate** the ancient burial site but found nothing of interest.

Exercise A: Synonyms

Write the word from the vocab list which is *most similar* in meaning next to each word listed below.

1. Unclear _____
2. Connotation_____
3. Unearth _____
4. Inherent _____
5. Morality _____
6. Predictable _____
7. Concur _____
8. Vital _____
9. Usefulness _____
10. Distressed _____

VOCAB 7 WORD BANK

Innate

Conscience

Utility

Incoherent

Fretful

Indispensable

Foreseeable

Overtone

Coincide

Excavate

Exercise B: Complete the sentence

Write the most suitable word from the vocab list in the spaces below. You might need to change the form of the word; for instance, walk might become walked.

1. The babysitter could not comfort the _____ and grizzly toddler, who had a high temperature.

2. The _____ of owning a mobile phone is taken for granted in modern society.

3. Burt's _____ explanation of the incident made no sense, so I decided to ignore him.

4. Whilst Lily was trying to be polite, her argument had an aggressive _____.

5. I have an _____ desire to read and learn about the world around me.

6. The employees' views do not always _____ with the wishes of the managers.

7. Alan's _____ expertise was valued by every member of the organisation.

8. It took the geologists months to _____ down to the seam of rare volcanic rock.

9. When war broke out, David refused to fight on account of his moral _____.

10. This crime was completely _____, and steps should have been taken to prevent it.

Exercise C: Complete the sentence

Select the most suitable word from the choices provided.

1. There was a strong _____ of regret in Amy's farewell speech.

    a. coincide   **b. overtone**   **c. foreseeable**

2. The researcher's study became an _____ resource for scientists everywhere.

    a. fretful   **b. incoherent**   **c. indispensable**

3. The wicked pirate showed a lack of _____ when he plundered and then sank the treasure ship.

    a. innate   **b. conscience**   **c. utility**

4. The soldiers were ordered to _____ a tunnel beneath enemy lines.

    a. excavate   **b. overtone**   **c. foreseeable**

5. My parents' days off rarely _____, so we never go on day trips all together.

    a. coincide   **b. incoherent**   **c. indispensable**

6. James had the quality of _____ goodness; he was incapable of being unkind.

    a. utility   **b. innate**   **c. overtone**

7. The children became worried and _____ during the fierce thunderstorm.

    a. coincide   **b. conscience**   **c. fretful**

8. My older sister plans to go to university in the _____ future.

    a. excavate   **b. innate**   **c. foreseeable**

9. The lecture given by the professor was _____ and badly prepared, so no one understood it.

    a. incoherent   **b. overtone**   **c. coincide**

10. The bored student wondered about the _____ of learning irregular Latin verbs.

    a. utility   **b. innate**   **c. fretful**

Vocabulary 8

Learn the words below and then answer the questions that follow!

1. **Bask** (v.): to laze, lounge, relax, enjoy.
    The tabby cat jumped onto the window ledge and settled down to **bask** in the afternoon sun.

2. **Span** (v.): to cover; to extend across; to form an arch over.
    Tower Bridge **spans** the River Thames and is an impressive 240m wide.

3. **Influx** (n.): the entry of numerous people or things; stream, flood.
    During the summer months there was an **influx** of tourists into the quiet seaside village.

4. **Inert** (adj.): motionless, stationary, inactive, unmoving.
    Lisa had the flu and spent the day lying **inert** in her bed, watching TV.

5. **Nuance** (n.): slight difference, trace, distinction, variation.
    The artist's portrait reflected every **nuance** of the model's expression.

6. **Correlation** (n.): relationship between two things; association, link.
    Researchers have discovered a **correlation** between the use of screens at bedtime and poor sleep quality.

7. **Concession** (n.): something granted in response to demands; compromise, adjustment.
    After a series of strikes, the government made many **concessions** to the workers.

8. **Offspring** (n.): children or young; result, product.
    The lioness would do anything to protect her **offspring** from predators.

9. **Candour** (n.): being open and honest; frankness, truth.
    Su-Yin's **candour** is one of her redeeming qualities; she always speaks her mind.

10. **Acquisition** (n.): something that has been obtained; addition, purchase, takeover.
    Isaac's **acquisition** of a new car means that he no longer has enough money to go on holiday.

Exercise A: Synonyms

Write the word from the vocab list which is *most similar* in meaning next to each word listed below.

1. Flood _____

2. Distinction _____

3. Compromise_____

4. Link _____

5. Stationary _____

6. Purchase _____

7. Frankness _____

8. Extend _____

9. Revel _____

10. Child _____

VOCAB 8 WORD BANK

Bask

Span

Influx

Inert

Nuance

Correlation

Concession

Offspring

Candour

Acquisition

Exercise B: Complete the sentence

Write the most suitable word from the vocab list in the spaces below. You might need to change the form of the word; for instance, walk might become walked.

1. After I tidied my room, Mum made a _____ and let me have some cola.

2. Jacob planned his trip to _____ three countries over two months.

3. A duck and her eight _____ have taken up residence at the pond in my local park.

4. Tom admitted with surprising _____ that he did not know his 10 times table.

5. Many doctors stress the _____ between smoking and lung cancer.

6. The museum's _____ of ancient artefacts is guaranteed to boost ticket sales.

7. The street performer stood _____ like a statue in front of his audience.

8. Marek loves to analyse every slight _____ of meaning in our conversation.

9. Due to the _____ of refugees, the food-bank charity asked for more volunteers to help out.

10. Janine could finally _____ in her success as a novelist, after many years spent working without recognition.

Exercise C: Complete the sentence

Select the most suitable word from the choices provided.

1. Researchers suggested a _____ between education and higher income.

   a. correlation   **b. concession**   **c. nuance**

2. The _____ of Instagram and WhatsApp by Facebook made it the most powerful social media empire in the world.

   a. offspring   **b. candour**   **c. acquisition**

3. The otters came ashore to _____ in the morning sunshine.

   a. influx   **b. bask**   **c. span**

4. After being given an anaesthetic, the dog lay _____ on the operating table.

   a. offspring   **b. inert**   **c. correlation**

5. The lawyer refused to allow any _____s, so the deal could not go ahead.

   a. concession   **b. influx**   **c. span**

6. "Our results this season have been very disappointing," commented the football manager, with _____.

   a. candour   **b. inert**   **c. span**

7. The new motorway _____s the entire width of the country.

   a. concession   **b. bask**   **c. span**

8. An _____ of fleas from Europe led to the Great Plague of London in 1665.

   a. influx   **b. candour**   **c. acquisition**

9. Guinea pigs usually have between two and five _____ in a litter.

   a. offspring   **b. correlation**   **c. concession**

10. Jasmine enjoyed hearing every subtle _____ of tone in the opera singer's voice.

    a. bask   **b. inert**   **c. nuance**

Vocabulary 9

Learn the words below and then answer the questions that follow!

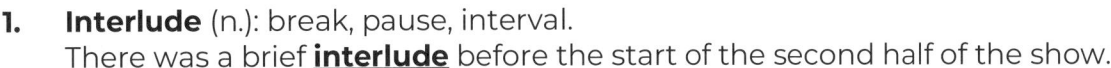

1. **Interlude** (n.): break, pause, interval.
    There was a brief **interlude** before the start of the second half of the show.

2. **Commentary** (n.): narration, description, account, explanation.
    Davina watched the movie with a **commentary** by the director, giving his opinion of each scene.

3. **Parasitic** (adj.): living as a parasite; taking advantage of; exploitative.
    My poor cat was given medication to clear it of a **parasitic** worm that was living in its intestines.

4. **Ephemeral** (adj.): lasting for an instant; fleeting, brief.
    The mayfly is the most **ephemeral** creature on earth; its lifespan is only 24 hours.

5. **Disconcerting** (adj.): worrying, alarming, troubling, unsettling.
    When we first drove our electric car, Mum found the lack of engine noise **disconcerting**.

6. **Patriarch** (n.): the male head of a family or tribe; father, leader.
    Traditionally, the leader of Eastern Orthodox churches has the title of **Patriarch**.

7. **Mildew** (n.): fungus, mould; a furry growth on damp materials.
    The flat had been abandoned and there was **mildew** growing on the walls.

8. **Provocation** (n.): an action that angers someone; incitement, molestation.
    Some nervous dogs can be alarmed at the slightest **provocation**.

9. **Medieval** (adj.): relating to the Middle Ages (10th to 15th century); old, archaic.
    The heavy, **medieval** armour was placed on display in the Museum of London.

10. **Illusory** (adj.): unreal, deceptive, imaginary.
    The magician's **illusory** techniques tricked the audience throughout his show.

Exercise A: Synonyms

Write the word from the vocab list which is *most similar* in meaning next to each word listed below.

1. Narration _____

2. Fleeting _____

3. Fungus _____

4. Archaic _____

5. Imaginary _____

6. Interval _____

7. Exploitative _____

8. Incitement _____

9. Alarming _____

10. Father _____

Exercise B: Complete the sentence

Write the most suitable word from the vocab list in the spaces below. You might need to change the form of the word; for instance, walk might become walked.

1. The _____ feast included a whole roast pig and boiled goose.

2. The plants had developed a white _____ which looked like a layer of snow.

3. The interior designer placed large mirrors around the house to give an _____ sense of space.

4. Remi is relaxed about his studies and did not find his bad exam results _____.

5. My great-grandfather was the _____ of the family, until he passed away.

6. I would not have understood the passage without a _____ from the professor.

7. The weather forecaster said it would rain all day, except for a sunny _____ at lunchtime.

8. I did not know that mistletoe is a _____ plant that grows on a host tree.

9. Ben lost his temper after extreme _____ by his bossy older sister.

10. People who become famous after being on reality TV often have short, _____ careers.

Exercise C: Complete the sentence

Select the most suitable word from the choices provided.

1. The _____ insects plagued all the cows on the farm.

    a. parasitic   **b. ephemeral**   **c. commentary**

2. The huge silverback was the _____ of the band of gorillas.

    a. mildew   **b. patriarch**   **c. disconcerting**

3. Logan has a seriously bad temper; he will snap at the slightest _____.

    a. medieval   **b. illusory**   **c. provocation**

4. The school play was extremely dramatic, so the parents welcomed the _____ and the chance for refreshments.

    a. mildew   **b. interlude**   **c. commentary**

5. The _____ cherry blossom season is celebrated in Japan with picnics under the trees.

    a. ephemeral   **b. parasitic**   **c. disconcerting**

6. There were patches of _____ on Joel's boots after he left them for months in the damp garage.

    a. patriarch   **b. mildew**   **c. illusory**

7. Salisbury Cathedral has been preserved for centuries and is a great example of _____ architecture.

    a. medieval   **b. interlude**   **c. commentary**

8. The lack of attention to global warming and climate change is _____.

    a. ephemeral   **b. patriarch**   **c. disconcerting**

9. Hopes for a peaceful resolution to the war were unrealistic and _____.

    a. illusory   **b. mildew**   **c. provocation**

10. Eddie provided an unnecessary _____ throughout the whole game of rugby.

    a. interlude   **b. parasitic**   **c. commentary**

Vocabulary 10

Learn the words below and then answer the questions that follow!

1. **Paradox** (n.): contradiction, inconsistency, absurdity, enigma.
   It is a **paradox** that many children still experience poverty in a wealthy country such as the UK.

2. **Seethe** (v.): to be angry or furious; to rage.
   Aisha failed to win the drama prize, which made her **seethe** with anger.

3. **Matinee** (n.): an afternoon/early performance in a theatre or cinema.
   Lesley could not attend the cinema in the evening, so she went to the **matinee** instead.

4. **Antiquated** (adj.): old-fashioned, outdated, archaic, outmoded.
   The **antiquated** boiler was on its last legs and broke down in the winter.

5. **Upturn** (n.): improvement, increase, rise, surge.
   After the investment of a million pounds, there was an **upturn** in the company's fortunes.

6. **Omniscient** (adj.): knowing everything; all-seeing, almighty.
   The book was written from the third-person perspective of an **omniscient** narrator.

7. **Import** (v.): to bring goods in from another country; to introduce a foreign idea.
   Britain has to **import** many of its raw materials from China.

8. **Niche** (adj.): appeal to a small, specific group of people; specialised, select.
   My friend David listens to a **niche**, little-known genre of rock music.

9. **Enclave** (n.): area, region; a part of a country surrounded by another country; a group of people who are ethnically or culturally different.
   The Vatican City is an **enclave** within the city of Rome.

10. **Inkling** (n.): suspicion, hint, impression, vague idea.
    I had an **inkling** that Rhys was the murderer when we were playing Cluedo.

Exercise A: Synonyms

Write the word from the vocab list which is *most similar* in meaning next to each word listed below.

1. Early performance_____

2. Specific   _____

3. Increase   _____

4. All-knowing_____

5. Old-fashioned_____

6. Rage   _____

7. Introduce   _____

8. Region   _____

9. Suspicion   _____

10. Contradiction_____

Exercise B: Complete the sentence

Write the most suitable word from the vocab list in the spaces below. You might need to change the form of the word; for instance, walk might become walked.

1. The tribe lived in a remote _____ in the jungle, cut off from the outside world.

2. It is difficult to _____ goods into the USA from Cuba due to a trade embargo.

3. Joe started to _____ when he found out he had been dropped from the first team.

4. There had been an _____ in the company's profits and the owner became very rich.

5. I prefer an evening show to a _____ because there are usually more people in the audience.

6. In the Bible, God is _____, so he knows everything and cannot be deceived.

7. Young people think that cheques are an _____ method of paying money.

8. Schrodinger's Cat is a famous _____ in physics that cannot be answered.

9. The organic supermarket sold specialised, _____ types of food.

10. I did not have any _____ that Teddy was the culprit behind the missing ball.

Exercise C: Complete the sentence

Select the most suitable word from the choices provided.

1. The footballers began to _____ with anger when they realised that their goal was disallowed.

   a. upturn   **b. seethe**   **c. enclave**

2. The _____ defences of the city were quickly destroyed by modern artillery.

   a. antiquated   **b. paradox**   **c. omniscient**

3. Sally could only get tickets for the _____ showing of the musical.

   a. antiquated   **b. matinee**   **c. niche**

4. The museum faced the _____ of having enormous wealth in treasures but not enough cash to pay its bills.

   a. paradox   **b. upturn**   **c. inkling**

5. The artist's work was described as _____ since his unique style was admired by very few people.

   a. omniscient   **b. niche**   **c. antiquated**

6. Since Brexit, it seems more complicated to _____ goods from Europe, because extra paperwork is required.

   a. import   **b. seethe**   **c. matinee**

7. Statistics showed a clear _____ in the children's exam results after new teaching techniques were used.

   a. paradox   **b. upturn**   **c. matinee**

8. Despite the good weather forecast, James had an _____ that it was going to rain.

   a. inkling   **b. enclave**   **c. omniscient**

9. Thousands of years ago, cavemen lived in a hidden _____ in the forest which provided both shelter and safety.

   a. inkling   **b. paradox**   **c. enclave**

10. Some people argue that public CCTV makes the government _____.

    a. omniscient   **b. seethe**   **c. import**

Vocabulary 11

Learn the words below and then answer the questions that follow!

1. **Tell-tale** (adj.): revealing, revelatory, indicative, suggestive.
   Mum spotted the **tell-tale** bulge of a packet of biscuits, which my sister had tried to hide under her jumper.

2. **Matriarch** (n.): a woman who is the head of a family or organisation.
   Aunt Brenda is considered the **matriarch** of our family, and everyone looks to her for advice.

3. **Pagan** (n.): someone who worships the earth or nature or who holds ancient but non-religious beliefs; heathen, atheistic.
   For an ancient **pagan**, Stonehenge may have been a place of worship or healing.

4. **Exponential** (adj.): increasing quickly by large amounts; growing, rampant.
   When Tarunjit became a teenager, he seemed to grow at an **exponential** rate.

5. **Remiss** (adj.): neglectful, careless, negligent, thoughtless.
   The babysitter was **remiss** in allowing the children to watch TV after their bedtime.

6. **Sprightly** (adj.): lively; full of energy (especially an old person).
   The winner of the race was a **sprightly** 80-year-old man.

7. **Viscous** (adj.): thick, gooey, slimy, syrupy.
   The **viscous** lava released by volcanoes in Hawaii destroyed many of the nearby villages.

8. **Irksome** (adj.): irritating, annoying, frustrating.
   Mrs Brown found the man's loud voice **irksome** as it prevented her from concentrating on her book.

9. **Cyclical** (adj.): occurring in cycles; periodic, seasonal.
   The changing of the seasons occurs every year in a **cyclical** manner.

10. **Pragmatic** (adj.): sensible, realistic, practical.
    President Obama took a **pragmatic** approach to the country's problems by listening to each side in turn.

Exercise A: Synonyms

Write the word from the vocab list which is *most similar* in meaning next to each word listed below.

1. Growing _____
2. Indicative _____
3. Periodic _____
4. Heathen _____
5. Syrupy _____
6. Mother _____
7. Practical _____
8. Frustrating _____
9. Lively _____
10. Careless _____

> VOCAB 11 WORD BANK
>
> Tell-tale
>
> Matriarch
>
> Pagan
>
> Exponential
>
> Remiss
>
> Sprightly
>
> Viscous
>
> Irksome
>
> Cyclical
>
> Pragmatic

Exercise B: Complete the sentence

Write the most suitable word from the vocab list in the spaces below. You might need to change the form of the word; for instance, walk might become walked.

1. It was _____ of Alice to forget to feed her hungry goldfish.

2. By creating a timetable, the student dealt with her revision in a _____ way.

3. In the past, _____s, or people with non-Christian beliefs, were considered inferior by the Church.

4. My granny is still _____ enough to enjoy skiing.

5. The empty biscuit tin was a _____ sign that Sam had been snacking.

6. The _____ growth of Apple as a company is mainly due to sales of the iPhone.

7. The surfers had to be aware of the _____ nature of the tides in Cornwall.

8. A combination of two chemicals produced a _____ liquid.

9. The duchess considered herself the _____ of the household, making all the financial decisions.

10. The commuters found the long queue at the station cafe _____ as they had a train to catch.

Exercise C: Complete the sentence

Select the most suitable word from the choices provided.

1. Some people do not like golden syrup with their pancakes because they find the consistency too _____.

   a. irksome   **b. viscous**   **c. exponential**

2. When Margaret Thatcher was elected as Prime Minister, her supporters saw her as the _____ of the country.

   a. matriarch   **b. pagan**   **c. tell-tale**

3. Mum found the crossword puzzle _____ as she could not solve the final question.

   a. cyclical   **b. irksome**   **c. remiss**

4. The angry passengers described the captain of the ship as _____ for failing to stop it sinking.

   a. pragmatic   **b. matriarch**   **c. remiss**

5. The Government attempted to find the most _____ approach to dealing with the energy crisis.

   a. pragmatic   **b. irksome**   **c. pagan**

6. The _____ stack of papers our teacher carried into the classroom indicated that there would be a test that morning.

   a. sprightly   **b. tell-tale**   **c. viscous**

7. The phases of the moon repeat in a _____ pattern.

   a. cyclical   **b. exponential**   **c. sprightly**

8. The _____ believed in the spiritual power of Nature.

   a. pagan   **b. matriarch**   **c. tell-tale**

9. My great-grandfather is very _____ and his favourite hobby is rock-climbing.

   a. remiss   **b. sprightly**   **c. irksome**

10. There has been an _____ increase in world population this century.

    a. exponential   **b. seethe**   **c. import**

Vocabulary 12

Learn the words below and then answer the questions that follow!

1. **Mania** (n.): fixation, compulsion, obsession, passion.
   During the 1960s, the band The Beatles caused a kind of **mania** amongst their obsessive fans.

2. **Writhe** (v.): to twist, squirm, wriggle.
   The rabbit began to **writhe** in fear as the vet started to examine him.

3. **Pious** (adj.): religious, dedicated, devout, godly.
   The **pious** girl was committed to attending church at least once a week.

4. **Antagonise** (v.): to make someone angry; to irritate, aggravate.
   Bullies often **antagonise** their victims with their hurtful actions.

5. **Wintry** (adj.): cold, chilly, frosty, snowy, bleak.
   In January, we braved the **wintry** weather to walk to school wearing boots and hats.

6. **Crag** (n.): steep, jagged mass of rock; peak, cliff, ridge.
   The climbers at last reached the **crag** at the top of the mountain.

7. **Eccentric** (adj.): unconventional, bizarre, unusual.
   I find my aunt's bright, multi-coloured outfits very **eccentric**.

8. **Premonition** (n.): a feeling that something is about to happen; suspicion, hunch.
   Jack awoke with a strong **premonition** that he was not going to pass his driving test.

9. **Lithe** (adj.): thin, flexible, graceful, agile.
   The professional dancer swept his partner up, in one **lithe** movement, and began to waltz around the ballroom.

10. **Intimacy** (n.): close and familiar relationship; familiarity.
    Shakespeare's play expresses a deep **intimacy** between the characters of Romeo and Juliet.

Exercise A: Synonyms

Write the word from the vocab list which is *most similar* in meaning next to each word listed below.

1. Frosty _____

2. Obsession _____

3. Unconventional_____

4. Cliff _____

5. Squirm _____

6. Feeling _____

7. Agile _____

8. Religious _____

9. Familiarity _____

10. Aggravate _____

VOCAB 12 WORD BANK

Mania

Writhe

Pious

Antagonise

Wintry

Crag

Eccentric

Premonition

Lithe

Intimacy

Exercise B: Complete the sentence

Write the most suitable word from the vocab list in the spaces below. You might need to change the form of the word; for instance, walk might become walked.

1. I had a _____ that I would win the lottery, but unfortunately it did not come true.

2. The pterodactyl built its nest high up on a snowy _____.

3. Uncle Jack had a complete _____ for fast cars.

4. Julie's thoughtful present for Harry showed the _____ between the two friends.

5. The king was a _____ man, dedicated to living his life by God's teachings.

6. Zachary had an _____ taste in music, listening to rap one minute and classical the next.

7. Mum tickled my little brother and he began to _____ with laughter.

8. To escape the _____ weather in December, my grandma booked a holiday to Jamaica.

9. The entrepreneur's erratic behaviour began to _____ his investors.

10. Auntie Beena still practises yoga regularly, so she is very _____ for her age.

Exercise C: Complete the sentence

Select the most suitable word from the choices provided.

1. From an early age, the _____ young man knew he wanted to become a priest.

    a. wintry   **b. pious**   **c. eccentric**

2. The headmaster managed to _____ many of the students by replacing chocolate desserts with fruit in the school canteen.

    a. antagonise   **b. writhe**   **c. pious**

3. Edinburgh Castle sits on Castle Rock, a _____ which dominates the city.

    a. lithe   **b. intimacy**   **c. crag**

4. Even as a child, the athlete had always spoken of his _____ that he would one day win a gold medal.

    a. mania   **b. premonition**   **c. lithe**

5. The snake started to _____ around when the charmer played his pipe.

    a. writhe   **b. antagonise**   **c. eccentric**

6. The _____ and stealthy cat stalked his prey, concealed by the bushes.

    a. premonition   **b. intimacy**   **c. lithe**

7. The atmospheric, old theatre had an _____ which was hard to match.

    a. intimacy   **b. mania**   **c. wintry**

8. Many children develop a kind of _____ over computer games such as Minecraft.

    a. mania   **b. eccentric**   **c. intimacy**

9. The artist's home had rather _____ furniture, including an emerald-green velvet sofa.

    a. wintry   **b. eccentric**   **c. pious**

10. John found the _____ Alps to be the perfect location for his skiing holiday.

    a. crag   **b. premonition**   **c. wintry**

Vocabulary 13

Learn the words below and then answer the questions that follow!

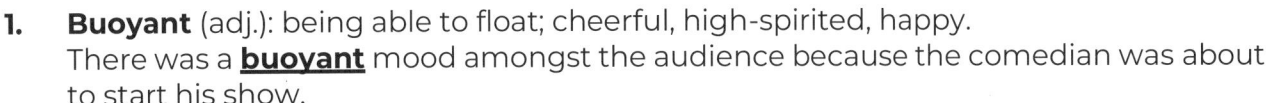

1. **Buoyant** (adj.): being able to float; cheerful, high-spirited, happy.
    There was a **buoyant** mood amongst the audience because the comedian was about to start his show.

2. **Reproach** (v.): to express disapproval or disappointment; to reprimand, criticise.
    The journalist **reproached** the government for its lack of a policy to help homeless people.

3. **Bashful** (adj.): shy, embarrassed, reserved, self-conscious.
    During my first day at school, I was too **bashful** to socialise and make new friends.

4. **Brimful** (adj.): full to the brim; almost overflowing.
    On the first day of the summer holidays the children were **brimful** of ideas as to what games they should play.

5. **Genesis** (n.): beginning, start; the beginning of existence.
    The **genesis** of my successful career as an actor came from one small part in a school play.

6. **Aflame** (adj.): on fire, burning, in flames.
    Many famous buildings were **aflame** during the Great Fire of London.

7. **Suggestive** (adj.): when something makes you think of something else; reminiscent, evocative.
    The doctor told us that my little sister's symptoms were **suggestive** of asthma.

8. **Glacial** (adj.): related to glaciers; frozen; very slow moving.
    Yasmin grew tired of waiting for a work promotion; her progress in the company seemed to be moving at a **glacial** pace.

9. **Quip** (n.): a witty, humorous remark; joke.
    My friend's **quip** about our strictest teacher made the whole class roar with laughter.

10. **Waive** (v.): to give up, forfeit, disregard, cancel.
    Vincent decided to **waive** his right to legal representation, because he wanted to represent himself in court.

Exercise A: Synonyms

Write the word from the vocab list which is *most similar* in meaning next to each word listed below.

1. Shy   _____
2. Joke   _____
3. Overflowing_____
4. Reminiscent_____
5. Criticise   _____
6. Frozen   _____
7. Forfeit   _____
8. Floating   _____
9. Beginning _____
10. Burning   _____

Exercise B: Complete the sentence

Write the most suitable word from the vocab list in the spaces below. You might need to change the form of the word; for instance, walk might become walked.

1. Some say that the invention of the radio was the _____ of modern music.

2. Mum gave Samuel one of her _____ stares across the table when he revealed he had been in trouble at school.

3. The Prime Minister answered the journalist's question with a clever _____.

4. Our local art gallery _____s the entry fee on Sundays.

5. The climbers' yawns were _____ of their complete exhaustion.

6. After receiving an expensive bicycle for his birthday, Dan was in a _____ mood.

7. For Mother's Day we presented Mum with a basket _____ of scented flowers.

8. Although a talented singer, the _____ girl felt too nervous to perform on stage.

9. Alf did not _____ Fran for being late as he knew her bus had broken down.

10. Annie's cheeks were _____ with embarrassment when she forgot her lines on stage.

Exercise C: Complete the sentence

Select the most suitable word from the choices provided.

1. The _____ coconut floated all the way from Hawaii to California.

    a. bashful   **b. buoyant**   **c. suggestive**

2. The grey clouds and crashing waves were _____ of the rough storm to come.

    a. suggestive   **b. brimful**   **c. genesis**

3. When suspects plead guilty to a charge they may _____ their right to appeal.

    a. waive   **b. quip**   **c. reproach**

4. The _____ boy looked embarrassed when the teacher told him to answer a question.

    a. buoyant   **b. bashful**   **c. aflame**

5. The forest fires in California had set entire villages _____, causing huge damage.

    a. aflame   **b. glacial**   **c. brimful**

6. Historians have traced the _____ of the English language back thousands of years.

    a. waive   **b. aflame**   **c. genesis**

7. Jen was offended when Jo made an unkind _____ about her new haircut.

    a. quip   **b. reproach**   **c. aflame**

8. A few schools undertake school trips to Iceland for geography students to see the _____ landscape.

    a. buoyant   **b. glacial**   **c. suggestive**

9. Eric's cousins were _____ of compliments at the end of his piano recital.

    a. brimful   **b. aflame**   **c. quip**

10. My parents _____ed me after the headmistress informed them that I had been caught cheating.

    a. waive   **b. reproach**   **c. quip**

Vocabulary 14

Learn the words below and then answer the questions that follow!

1. **Genteel** (adj.): polite, well-mannered, cultured.
   In traditional fairy tales, the hero is often described as a **genteel** prince who rescues the princess.

2. **Quizzical** (adj.): baffled, questioning, puzzled, curious.
   The detective evaluated the suspects with a **quizzical** gaze.

3. **Spiny** (adj.): covered with spines; prickly, spiky.
   When I fell on a **spiny** cactus, it took the doctor three hours to remove all the needles from my hands.

4. **Irresolute** (adj.): unable to make up your mind; uncertain, doubtful.
   Our government seems **irresolute** and inactive on almost every important issue.

5. **Upbraid** (v.): to criticise, scold, reprimand, blame.
   The music teacher had to **upbraid** Dylan in front of the whole class, due to his disruptive behaviour.

6. **Uppermost** (adj.): highest, most important, paramount.
   The celebrity's wedding cake had ten layers; the **uppermost** was sprinkled with gold leaf.

7. **Berth** (n): a place where a ship is tied up in a port; a bed or bunk in a boat, caravan or train.
   The captain spent hours choosing the perfect **berth** in which to moor his prized ship.

8. **Feign** (v.): to pretend to do something to divert attention; to deceive, bluff.
   When taking a penalty, the striker may **feign** his next move by looking to the left then kicking the ball to the right, to deceive the goalkeeper.

9. **Calorie** (n.): a unit used to describe the amount of energy in food.
   Dieticians recommend a **calorie**-controlled diet to help lose weight.

10. **Euphemism** (n.): a word or phrase which is used to avoid saying something rude or blunt; a mild alternative, understatement.
    James said his uncle was 'big-boned', but we all knew this was a **euphemism,** meaning fat.

Exercise A: Synonyms

Write the word from the vocab list which is *most similar* in meaning next to each word listed below.

1. Questioning _____
2. Criticise _____
3. Uncertain _____
4. Understatement _____
5. Polite _____
6. Unit of energy _____
7. Prickly _____
8. Pretend _____
9. Highest _____
10. Bunk _____

VOCAB 14 WORD
BANK

Genteel

Quizzical

Spiny

Irresolute

Upbraid

Uppermost

Berth

Feign

Calorie

Euphemism

Exercise B: Complete the sentence

Write the most suitable word from the vocab list in the spaces below. You might need to change the form of the word; for instance, walk might become walked.

1. The fisherman found the _____ crab extremely difficult to pick up.

2. Julia loved her flat on the _____ floor of the apartment block, as it had views right across London.

3. Hermione wrote a letter to the headmistress to _____ the school on its wasteful use of plastic.

4. We are only allowed jam doughnuts once a week due to their high _____ content.

5. When her family took the night train to Edinburgh, Iona asked if she could sleep on

   the upper _____.

6. The pupil gave Mr Smith a _____ look after being asked a difficult algebra question.

7. 'Senior citizens' is a common _____ for the less polite phrase, 'old people'.

8. Jack _____ed an illness to miss school.

9. The Victorian house had retained its _____ and elegant interior.

10. I stood at the front door, _____ and undecided about whether to knock.

Exercise C: Complete the sentence

Select the most suitable word from the choices provided.

1. One of the hardest parts of being in the Navy is having to sleep in a narrow _____ on a ship.

    a. calorie   **b. berth**   **c. upbraid**

2. I was encouraged by my family to use the _____ 'passed away' instead of 'died'.

    a. irresolute   **b. feign**   **c. euphemism**

3. During the dinner party, the guests were polite and behaved in a _____ manner.

    a. genteel   **b. spiny**   **c. quizzical**

4. Maddy gave the wrapped presents a _____ look as she tried to predict what they might be.

    a. irresolute   **b. feign**   **c. quizzical**

5. Hedgehogs are _____ to protect them from potential predators.

    a. genteel   **b. spiny**   **c. uppermost**

6. After leaving school, Paulo was _____ and aimless, not knowing which career to aim for.

    a. irresolute   **b. uppermost**   **c. spiny**

7. I thought Mum would _____ me for taking the last chip, but she did not notice.

    a. upbraid   **b. berth**   **c. irresolute**

8. The breakfast cereal manufacturer changed its recipes to reduce the _____ content of products aimed at children.

    a. calorie   **b. berth**   **c. euphemism**

9. The boxer managed to outwit his opponent by _____ing an injury and then fighting back.

    a. quizzical   **b. feign**   **c. upbraid**

10. Doing homework was not _____ in Liam's mind and he started playing his new computer game instead.

    a. irresolute   **b. spiny**   **c. uppermost**

Vocabulary 15

Learn the words below and then answer the questions that follow!

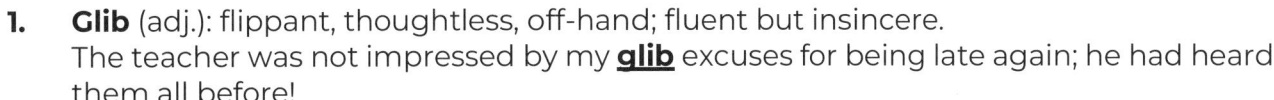

1. **Glib** (adj.): flippant, thoughtless, off-hand; fluent but insincere.
   The teacher was not impressed by my **glib** excuses for being late again; he had heard them all before!

2. **Prejudice** (n.): unfair, judgemental opinion; preconception, bias.
   Dad has a **prejudice** against Alsatian dogs because one knocked him over when he was a toddler.

3. **Impartial** (adj.): fair-minded, unprejudiced, neutral, objective.
   I did not take sides and remained **impartial** when my two closest friends got into an argument.

4. **Franchise** (n.): permission to sell another company's products; a permit, authorisation, licence.
   One of the major train companies lost its **franchise** due to so many complaints.

5. **Languish** (v.): to weaken, decline, deteriorate; to be neglected.
   When my sister lost her sleeping bag on the camping trip, she was forced to **languish** under a thin blanket in the cold.

6. **Autocrat** (n.): domineering ruler; dictator, tyrant
   Under the evil **autocrat**, the citizens had very few rights or freedoms.

7. **Animosity** (n): strong dislike, hostility, resentment, enmity.
   After Chris carelessly broke his brother's guitar, there was a great deal of **animosity** between the two.

8. **Fulfilment** (n.): feeling of satisfaction, contentment.
   Margaret found more **fulfilment** in her new job as an artist than as an office worker.

9. **Reprimand** (v.): to rebuke, scold, criticise, tell off.
   The headmistress had to **reprimand** Nora after she was caught talking during assembly.

10. **Delegate** (n.): representative, envoy, agent, deputy.
    Each country will send a **delegate** to the international climate change meeting.

Exercise A: Synonyms

Write the word from the vocab list which is *most similar* in meaning next to each word listed below.

	VOCAB 15 WORD BANK	

Glib

Prejudice

Impartial

Franchise

Languish

Autocrat

Animosity

Fulfilment

Reprimand

Delegate

1. Licence _____

2. Hostility _____

3. Suffer _____

4. Criticise _____

5. Flippant _____

6. Dictator _____

7. Bias _____

8. Satisfaction _____

9. Representative_____

10. Neutral _____

Exercise B: Complete the sentence

Write the most suitable word from the vocab list in the spaces below. You might need to change the form of the word; for instance, walk might become walked.

1. The judge instructed the jury to be _____ and base their decision only on the evidence.

2. Jasdeep felt a great sense of _____ after reaching the summit of the mountain.

3. The con-man was excellent at deceiving people with his _____ comments.

4. The politician was a crafty _____ who made every important decision without consulting others.

5. Governments must not hold _____ towards any groups in society as this may lead to unfair treatment.

6. I act as a _____ for my school year group on the student council.

7. Our local car dealership was granted the _____ to sell Toyota models.

8. The teacher decided to _____ the disrespectful child in front of everyone.

9. There was a palpable sense of _____ before the match between two rival rugby teams.

10. Pablo had left the novel to _____ unread on the shelf.

Exercise C: Complete the sentence

Select the most suitable word from the choices provided.

1. In Britain we have public elections so that no politician can act as an _____.

    a. prejudice   **b. franchise**   **c. autocrat**

2. Nowadays, video recordings are used to check that football referees make _____ decisions.

    a. glib   **b. impartial**   **c. languish**

3. Our team is out of the cup tournament as they currently _____ at the bottom of the league tables.

    a. languish   **b. autocrat**   **c. animosity**

4. The _____ between the two countries made peace almost impossible.

    a. animosity   **b. franchise**   **c. reprimand**

5. When the company lost its _____ to sell Oreo biscuits, sales fell massively.

    a. impartial   **b. franchise**   **c. delegate**

6. Politicians often fill their speeches with _____ promises which sound great but are never delivered.

    a. impartial   **b. fulfilment**   **c. glib**

7. Betty finally found _____ in life when she started helping at the shelter for abandoned animals.

    a. fulfilment   **b. languish**   **c. animosity**

8. Each _____ at the conference had the chance to put their views across.

    a. autocrat   **b. reprimand**   **c. delegate**

9. Even today, some women can come up against _____ in the workplace.

    a. prejudice   **b. impartial**   **c. franchise**

10. Dad had to _____ my sister for cheating at our family game of Monopoly.

    a. prejudice   **b. glib**   **c. reprimand**

Vocabulary 16

Learn the words below and then answer the questions that follow!

1. **Deranged** (adj.): insane, crazed, unstable.
   Several players were injured by the **deranged** football fan who threw glass bottles onto the pitch.

2. **Implication** (n.): suggestion, hint, inference, insinuation.
   When Justin Bieber stated that there were surprises in store for his fans, the **implication** was that he would release a new album.

3. **Subordinate** (adj.): of lesser importance or rank; junior, inferior, secondary.
   The role of Vice-President is **subordinate** to that of the President.

4. **Acquire** (v.): to gain possession of; to buy, purchase, procure.
   Lisa hoped to **acquire** a red Porsche after passing her driving test.

5. **Assassinate** (v.): to kill (often someone famous or important); to murder, execute.
   The police have foiled many attempts to **assassinate** the King.

6. **Endure** (v.): to experience, suffer, bear, tolerate.
   Britain had to **endure** over a decade of food rationing during and after World War Two.

7. **Flatten** (v): to level, smooth, compress, squash.
   Leo attempted to **flatten** his untidy hair, which was sticking up as usual.

8. **Mould** (v.): to shape, change, create, sculpt.
   The jeweller tried to **mould** an exact replica of the prince's gold medallion.

9. **Undisturbed** (adj.): uninterrupted, peaceful, tranquil.
   The island was left **undisturbed** for many years, which allowed its beauty to flourish without pollution.

10. **Cram** (v.): to force into; to overfill, squash, pack.
    The farmer had to **cram** all his sheep into a barn to protect them from a storm.

Exercise A: Synonyms

Write the word from the vocab list which is *most similar* in meaning next to each word listed below.

	VOCAB 16 WORD BANK

VOCAB 16 WORD BANK

Deranged

Implication

Subordinate

Acquire

Assassinate

Endure

Flatten

Mould

Undisturbed

Cram

1. Purchase _____

2. Insane _____

3. Level _____

4. Uninterrupted_____

5. Suggestion _____

6. Shape _____

7. Inferior _____

8. Overfill _____

9. Suffer _____

10. Murder _____

Exercise B: Complete the sentence

Write the most suitable word from the vocab list in the spaces below. You might need to change the form of the word; for instance, walk might become walked.

1. The ghost story featuring a _____ old lady gave the children nightmares for weeks.

2. The approaching hurricane is likely to _____ the famous botanical gardens.

3. In Maggie's first job she held a _____ position but eventually she became the managing director.

4. Jennifer asked Mum to _____ roses out of icing, to decorate her birthday cake.

5. The sniper wanted to _____ the princess, but luckily he was caught in time.

6. Jacob hoped to _____ a Picasso painting during the upcoming gallery auction.

7. Lucas had to _____ his hamster into his pocket when the cat appeared.

8. When my brother said the film had been 'average', the _____ was that he had not enjoyed it very much.

9. The tombs in Egypt were left _____ for thousands of years before archaeologists finally discovered them.

10. The bus passengers had to _____ an hour-long traffic-jam, many without a seat.

Exercise C: Complete the sentence

Select the most suitable word from the choices provided.

1. The poet chose to live _____ in the mountains, where he could focus on writing without interruption.

    a. deranged   **b. undisturbed**   **c. cram**

2. The soldiers had to obey their commander, as they were _____ to him.

    a. flatten   **b. endure**   **c. subordinate**

3. Sarah sacrificed all her pocket-money to _____ the latest high-tech skateboard.

    a. acquire   **b. assassinate**   **c. endure**

4. Schools can help to _____ the personalities and behaviour of their pupils.

    a. deranged   **b. subordinate**   **c. mould**

5. My sister thinks I am _____ because I love cauliflower with ketchup on it.

    a. deranged   **b. undisturbed**   **c. subordinate**

6. Mary Queen of Scots plotted to _____ Queen Elizabeth I.

    a. assassinate   **b. implication**   **c. mould**

7. Before going on holiday, Bella had to _____ five injections to protect her from tropical diseases.

    a. cram   **b. endure**   **c. flatten**

8. The rhinoceros's heavy feet managed to _____ all the plants in its path.

    a. mould   **b. acquire**   **c. flatten**

9. When Tim blushed and started to stammer, the _____ was that he felt embarrassed.

    a. subordinate   **b. implication**   **c. assassinate**

10. Some lucky members of the audience were allowed to _____ into the space next to the stage, right in front of the singer.

    a. acquire   **b. cram**   **c. deranged**

Vocabulary 17

Learn the words below and then answer the questions that follow!

1. **Procure** (v.): to acquire, obtain, buy; to gain possession of something.
   Dad was ecstatic when he managed to **procure** tickets for the cup final.

2. **Makeshift** (adj.): improvised, substitute, temporary.
   The scouts' **makeshift** tent, constructed from plastic sheets and branches, provided basic shelter.

3. **Wander** (v.): to roam, amble, drift; to walk aimlessly.
   Tilly loved nothing better than to **wander** over the hills taking photos of wildflowers.

4. **Wary** (adj.): careful, alert, prudent, cautious.
   Ella was **wary** of getting too close to the frisky horses because she did not want to excite them further.

5. **Particularly** (adv.): especially, very, mainly.
   My waterproof trousers were **particularly** useful on our school camping trip.

6. **Insurance** (n.): compensation, security, financial protection, back-up.
   We were refunded when our flight was cancelled because we had purchased travel **insurance**.

7. **Bayonet** (n.): a stabbing blade fixed to a rifle; spear, harpoon.
   Every soldier in WWI was armed with a **bayonet** and a rifle.

8. **Panic** (v.): to feel afraid, terrified or alarmed; to take fright.
   Julia began to **panic** when she realised that her exams were merely days away.

9. **Uncomfortable** (adj.): awkward, tense, uneasy, embarrassed.
   The young boy felt shy and **uncomfortable** when the teacher read his poem aloud to the whole class.

10. **Weep** (v.): to cry uncontrollably, sob, shed tears.
    When the heroine died tragically at the end of the play, the entire audience began to **weep**.

Exercise A: Synonyms

Write the word from the vocab list which is *most similar* in meaning next to each word listed below.

1. Cautious _____
2. Blade _____
3. Especially _____
4. Temporary _____
5. Awkward _____
6. Roam _____
7. Take fright _____
8. Sob _____
9. Safeguard _____
10. Obtain _____

VOCAB 17 WORD BANK

Procure

Makeshift

Wander

Wary

Particularly

Insurance

Bayonet

Panic

Uncomfortable

Weep

Exercise B: Complete the sentence

Write the most suitable word from the vocab list in the spaces below. You might need to change the form of the word; for instance, walk might become walked.

1. Little Oscar began to _____ and wail, after Mum said he could not have an ice cream.

2. It was difficult to _____ tickets for the music festival because it was so popular.

3. The rabbits appeared very _____ of us and hopped away as we approached.

4. Maria's dad was relieved that he had _____ after his car was crushed by a falling tree.

5. A _____ blade is made of a strong metal such as steel.

6. The cattle are allowed to _____ freely over the great plain.

7. I _____ enjoyed looking at the paintings by Monet in the National Gallery.

8. After the tsunami, refugees were forced to live in _____ camps for many months.

9. Adam felt very _____ as he knew his friend Billy had lied to the sports coach.

10. The bridesmaids began to _____ when they realised they had lost the bride's flowers.

Exercise C: Complete the sentence

Select the most suitable word from the choices provided.

1. The expert valued the antique rifle highly because the _____ was still attached.

    a. bayonet   **b. weep**   **c. insurance**

2. When our home was burgled, we claimed for the stolen goods through our _____.

    a. panic   **b. wary**   **c. insurance**

3. The entire community began to _____ when it was announced that a puma had escaped from the zoo.

    a. wander   **b. uncomfortable**   **c. panic**

4. The strange look in Bob's eyes made me _____ about agreeing to his plan.

    a. wary   **b. insurance**   **c. bayonet**

5. After the flood, our school hall was turned into a _____ shelter.

    a. makeshift   **b. wary**   **c. weep**

6. Emily felt very _____ during the camel ride, due to the lumpy saddle.

    a. wander   **b. makeshift**   **c. uncomfortable**

7. The discount voucher entitled us to _____ two pizzas for the price of one.

    a. procure   **b. bayonet**   **c. insurance**

8. The hikers started to _____ away from the trail, and they soon became lost.

    a. panic   **b. particularly**   **c. wander**

9. My little sister began to _____ after she dropped her teddy bear in a puddle.

    a. wander   **b. weep**   **c. uncomfortable**

10. Our class is _____ excited about entering Year 5 because we will go on a trip to the Isle of Wight.

    a. procure   **b. particularly**   **c. wary**

Vocabulary 18

Learn the words below and then answer the questions that follow!

1. **Decency** (n.): good manners, courtesy, respect.
   My brother had the **decency** to apologise after he forgot my birthday.

2. **Capable** (adj.): competent, efficient, skilful, effective.
   Thomas's delicious brownies proved that he was a **capable** baker.

3. **Tender** (adj.): gentle, loving, kind; painful, sensitive.
   After I fell asleep in the sun, my burned legs remained **tender** for several days.

4. **Grimace** (v.): to scowl, frown; to pull a face, expressing disgust, pain etc.
   Mia started to **grimace** with pain as she stood up on her twisted ankle.

5. **Skim** (v.): to move lightly across the top of something; to read quickly through a text.
   I saw an eagle **skim** the surface of the lake, barely touching the water, and catch a fish with its claws.

6. **Whirl** (v.): to spin around, twist rapidly, twirl.
   The dancers had to **whirl** around the ballroom until the music stopped.

7. **Clank** (v.): to make the sound of metal hitting metal; to clang, clash, clatter.
   I could hear the saucepans **clank** and clatter noisily as Dad tidied up the kitchen.

8. **Scamper** (v.): to run with quick and light steps; to scuttle, scurry, dash.
   I noticed a rat **scamper** rapidly through the back alley, heading for the sewers.

9. **Exaggerate** (v.): to make something seem bigger or better than it is; to magnify, overstate.
   Henry tended to **exaggerate** his abilities in everything because he was rather big-headed.

10. **Bolt** (v.): to run, dash, sprint, hurry.
    The robber had to **bolt** towards the exit before the security guards could catch him.

Exercise A: Synonyms

Write the word from the vocab list which is *most similar* in meaning next to each word listed below.

1. Gentle _____

2. Clatter _____

3. Overstate _____

4. Courtesy _____

5. Scuttle _____

6. Sweep _____

7. Scowl _____

8. Sprint _____

9. Competent _____

10. Twirl _____

VOCAB 18 WORD BANK

Decency

Capable

Tender

Grimace

Skim

Whirl

Clank

Scamper

Exaggerate

Bolt

Exercise B: Complete the sentence

Write the most suitable word from the vocab list in the spaces below. You might need to change the form of the word; for instance, walk might become walked.

1. David Beckham was highly _____ at football even at a young age.

2. Paula was successful in English comprehension tests as she had learned to _____ the text quickly but thoroughly.

3. Ellie tried not to _____ at the awful sound of the dentist's drill.

4. People began to _____ at top speed towards the shop when they realised prices had been slashed.

5. The entire world appeared to _____ past me as I spun on the roundabout.

6. Despite all the evidence, some people say that scientists _____ the effects of global warming.

7. It is seen as basic _____ to be polite to people.

8. The bike lock started to rattle and _____ when the thief tried to break it off.

9. The puppy tried to _____ up the slide, but it was too slippery.

10. I gave my baby brother a _____, loving look before rocking him to sleep.

Exercise C: Complete the sentence

Select the most suitable word from the choices provided.

1. Andy's mother would always _____ in disgust at the mess and clutter in his room.

   a. scamper   **b. exaggerate**   **c. grimace**

2. The teenage girl had little common _____, as she refused to give up her seat for an elderly lady on the train.

   a. tender   **b. decency**   **c. clank**

3. The fox loves to _____ through the undergrowth at the bottom of our garden.

   a. scamper   **b. whirl**   **c. grimace**

4. When the duck landed on the water, it barely seemed to _____ the surface.

   a. skim   **b. capable**   **c. bolt**

5. We live near the station and I can hear the trains _____ as they pull out in the morning.

   a. scamper   **b. decency**   **c. clank**

6. Mum said I might be _____ of becoming an author one day as I invent so many imaginative stories.

   a. capable   **b. exaggerate**   **c. whirl**

7. The bruise on my arm was still _____ two weeks after the accident.

   a. clank   **b. bolt**   **c. tender**

8. The pointed shoes seemed to _____ the size of my feet.

   a. exaggerate   **b. skim**   **c. grimace**

9. A tornado continued to _____ through the state of California, causing damage and destruction.

   a. whirl   **b. tender**   **c. capable**

10. The children _____ed through the woods as fast as they could away from the spooky haunted house.

   a. clank   **b. bolt**   **c. skim**

Vocabulary 19

Learn the words below and then answer the questions that follow!

1. **Cower** (v.): to crouch down in fear; to flinch, pull away, recoil.
   The puppy **cowered** as its owner screamed and shouted in rage.

2. **Stammer** (v.): to stutter, hesitate, stumble over words.
   My sister Talia often starts to **stammer** when she is nervous and struggles to speak in public.

3. **Gesture** (n.): movement, signal, action, deed.
   When her friend began to cry, Amelia gave her a hug as a **gesture** of kindness and support.

4. **Flurry** (n.): swirling mass of something; sudden, short period of activity.
   A **flurry** of snow had blown into our tent and soaked our sleeping bags.

5. **Infrastructure** (n.): the basic services or framework of an institution or country.
   Some poorer countries are in desperate need of basic **infrastructure** such as railway networks.

6. **Senseless** (adj.): futile, pointless, useless; unconscious, stunned.
   The cat killed all the baby birds in the nest, which was a **senseless** waste of life.

7. **Triumphantly** (adv.): in a way that shows great happiness, joy or pride, e.g. after a victory or achievement.
   The athlete **triumphantly** accepted his gold medal after winning the race.

8. **Blueprint** (n.): technical drawing, plan, diagram, design, map.
   The builders followed the **blueprint** to construct the new skyscraper.

9. **Squadron** (n.): group or unit within the armed forces; squad, troop, crew.
   During World War II, Russia had an all-female **squadron** of fighter pilots.

10. **Mountainous** (adj.): area with lots of mountains; hilly, rocky.
    Eagles often build their nests in high, **mountainous** areas, where they are safe from predators.

Exercise A: Synonyms

Write the word from the vocab list which is *most similar* in meaning next to each word listed below.

1. Services   _____

2. Recoil   _____

3. Unit   _____

4. Stutter   _____

5. Proudly   _____

6. Swirl   _____

7. Plan   _____

8. Hilly   _____

9. Movement   _____

10. Pointless   _____

VOCAB 19 WORD BANK

Cower

Stammer

Gesture

Flurry

Infrastructure

Senseless

Triumphantly

Blueprint

Squadron

Mountainous

Exercise B: Complete the sentence

Write the most suitable word from the vocab list in the spaces below. You might need to change the form of the word; for instance, walk might become walked.

1. Amir had a tendency to _____ nervously whenever the teacher asked him a question in class.

2. The new Prime Minister _____ delivered her winning speech.

3. When asked to point out her favourite toy, the little girl made a _____ towards a tiny, pink rabbit.

4. After the floods, much of Cornwall's road and rail _____ was destroyed.

5. The video game involved two air _____s battling against one another.

6. My dog is very nervous and will often _____ behind me if she encounters another, larger dog.

7. Nepal is a _____ region, made up of many small villages and rough terrain.

8. The gust of wind sent a _____ of leaves whirling to the ground.

9. The champion boxer knocked his opponent _____.

10. When examining the _____ of the building, the detective found a secret passageway.

Exercise C: Complete the sentence

Select the most suitable word from the choices provided.

1. The politician said that the new office building was a _____ waste of money.

    a. squadron   **b. senseless**   **c. flurry**

2. Ali offered us some homemade cookies, which was a very friendly _____.

    a. gesture   **b. stammer**   **c. infrastructure**

3. Jasmine smiled _____ as she realised her painting had won the art prize.

    a. senseless   **b. stammer**   **c. triumphantly**

4. The charity is building new _____ to provide the remote island with clean drinking water.

    a. infrastructure   **b. senseless**   **c. mountainous**

5. The citizens _____ed in their homes as the victorious army looted the city.

    a. senseless   **b. cower**   **c. triumphantly**

6. The burglar studied the _____ of the bank in order to locate the safe.

    a. gesture   **b. blueprint**   **c. flurry**

7. There was a _____ of goodbyes as the family set off late for the airport.

    a. flurry   **b. infrastructure**   **c. mountainous**

8. Theo thought he saw a ghost, so he turned pale and began to _____.

    a. stammer   **b. flurry**   **c. squadron**

9. Carla emerged from the library with a _____ stack of books to read over her summer holiday.

    a. gesture   **b. stammer**   **c. mountainous**

10. The helicopter _____ was given a mission to drop food packages over a remote region cut off by the storms.

    a. blueprint   **b. squadron**   **c. triumphantly**

Vocabulary 20

Learn the words below and then answer the questions that follow!

1. **Leaden** (adj.): heavy, lead-coloured, dull grey.
   The gloomy, **leaden** sky began to erupt with thunder and lightning.

2. **Buckle** (v.): to collapse under pressure; to bend, snap, warp.
   As the heavy lorries drove over it, the bridge started to **buckle** and weaken.

3. **Mournfully** (adv.): sadly, woefully, gloomily, unhappily.
   David **mournfully** said goodbye to his friend, who was moving to Australia.

4. **Singular** (adj.): outstanding, unusual, exceptional; single, unique, alone.
   The girl showed a **singular** talent for the violin, quickly mastering grade five.

5. **Incendiary** (adj.): likely to stir up conflict, provocative, inflammatory; designed to cause fires, flammable.
   The protesters were arrested after police discovered a homemade **incendiary** bomb in their car.

6. **Ravenous** (adj.): very hungry, starving.
   The lioness was **ravenous** after failing to catch any prey for several days.

7. **Plateau** (n.): area of flat, high ground, plain; stable period of no change.
   The athlete's speed improved week after week, until his progress reached a **plateau** and he could run no faster.

8. **Beloved** (adj.): dearly loved, adored, precious.
   Queen Elizabeth II's **beloved** husband of many years was called Prince Philip.

9. **Credentials** (n.): qualifications, achievements; qualities that show a person's ability to fulfil a role.
   Before being hired as Chief of Police, Sachin's **credentials** were checked to ensure that he had the right skills for the job.

10. **Harried** (adj.): worried, stressed, pressured, agitated.
    The **harried** teacher glanced nervously at the pile of test papers, which needed to be marked urgently.

Exercise A: Synonyms

Write the word from the vocab list which is *most similar* in meaning next to each word listed below.

1. Starving _____
2. Weighty _____
3. Inflammatory _____
4. Precious _____
5. Unusual _____
6. Collapse _____
7. Qualifications _____
8. Sadly _____
9. Plain _____
10. Worried _____

VOCAB 20 WORD BANK

Leaden

Buckle

Mournfully

Singular

Incendiary

Ravenous

Plateau

Beloved

Credentials

Harried

Exercise B: Complete the sentence

Write the most suitable word from the vocab list in the spaces below. You might need to change the form of the word; for instance, walk might become walked.

1. George gazed _____ out of the plane window; he was already missing his puppy and the holiday had barely started.

2. After the lively toddlers went to sleep, the _____ babysitter was finally able to relax.

3. Survivors were left with serious burns caused by _____ weapons used during the attack.

4. After one heavy blow, the boxer felt his knees _____ and he fell to the floor.

5. Paul's stomach rumbled and he cast a _____ look at the delicious food his grandma had cooked.

6. People considered the actor to be an unusual and _____ character.

7. My eyelids were _____ with sleep and I could not keep them open any longer.

8. Matilda snuggled up every night with her _____ cuddly toys.

9. Neil Armstrong had the perfect background and _____ to be an astronaut.

10. Dad said that house prices had reached a _____ and would not increase any further.

Exercise C: Complete the sentence

Select the most suitable word from the choices provided.

1. Mrs Shah refused to employ a plumber unless she had seen their _____, proving they were fully qualified.

   a. incendiary   **b. beloved**   **c. credentials**

2. Cheetahs are known for their _____ ability to run faster than any other land animal.

   a. ravenous   **b. singular**   **c. harried**

3. The _____ stray cat had not eaten for days, so it wolfed down the tinned food.

   a. plateau   **b. ravenous**   **c. singular**

4. The two brothers hugged one another _____ as the eldest prepared to leave the family home.

   a. mournfully   **b. harried**   **c. leaden**

5. Ralph's career had reached a _____; he had been head chef for ten years and was unlikely to change jobs.

   a. plateau   **b. credentials**   **c. singular**

6. The car bumper _____d when the van crashed into it.

   a. mournfully   **b. ravenous**   **c. buckle**

7. Harriet purchased a gold collar as a birthday present for her _____ cat.

   a. buckle   **b. harried**   **c. beloved**

8. The virus made Millie's head feel _____ and her throat sore.

   a. leaden   **b. incendiary**   **c. mournfully**

9. Henry made an _____ comment during the argument and caused anger amongst his friends.

   a. incendiary   **b. plateau**   **c. credentials**

10. The _____ journalist could not finish his article in time for the publication date.

   a. singular   **b. harried**   **c. mournfully**

Answers

Vocabulary 1

Exercise A

1. Grievous
2. Heritage
3. Possessive
4. Indestructible
5. Accumulate
6. Comprehensive
7. Keepsake
8. Contradict
9. Advisory
10. Immoral

Exercise B

1. Possessive
2. Indestructible
3. Advisory
4. Comprehensive
5. Contradict
6. Keepsake
7. Accumulate
8. Heritage
9. Grievous
10. Immoral

Exercise C

1. Accumulate
2. Comprehensive
3. Immoral
4. Heritage
5. Possessive
6. Keepsake
7. Contradict
8. Indestructible
9. Grievous
10. Advisory

Vocabulary 2

Exercise A

1. Partially
2. Deceive
3. Pedestal
4. Obstinate
5. Negotiate
6. Characterise
7. Moderation
8. Implausible
9. Immeasurable
10. Enthusiastic

Exercise B

1. Pedestal
2. Implausible
3. Characterise
4. Obstinate
5. Enthusiastic
6. Deceive
7. Partially
8. Immeasurable
9. Negotiate
10. Moderation

Exercise C

1. Immeasurable
2. Characterise
3. Partially
4. Negotiate
5. Implausible
6. Obstinate
7. Moderation
8. Deceive
9. Enthusiastic
10. Pedestal

Vocabulary 3

Exercise A

1. Illicit
2. Liable
3. Stimulant
4. Mesmerise
5. Incomprehensible
6. Overdose
7. Terminus
8. Self-defence
9. Invariably
10. Hereditary

Exercise B

1. Terminus
2. Self-defence
3. Overdose
4. Liable
5. Hereditary
6. Stimulant
7. Invariably
8. Mesmerise
9. Incomprehensible
10. Illicit

Exercise C

1. Liable
2. Illicit
3. Mesmerise
4. Incomprehensible
5. Hereditary
6. Self-defence
7. Invariably
8. Terminus
9. Stimulant
10. Overdose

Answers

Vocabulary 4

Exercise A

1. Irreparable
2. Illogical
3. Profession
4. Insatiable
5. Manoeuvre
6. Palpable
7. Morose
8. Arbitrary
9. Zealous
10. Inseparable

Exercise B

1. Insatiable
2. Manoeuvre
3. Inseparable
4. Arbitrary
5. Illogical
6. Palpable
7. Morose
8. Profession
9. Irreparable
10. Zealous

Exercise C

1. Profession
2. Zealous
3. Palpable
4. Insatiable
5. Manoeuvre
6. Arbitrary
7. Irreparable
8. Morose
9. Illogical
10. Inseparable

Vocabulary 5

Exercise A

1. Mentality
2. Simultaneous
3. Affirmative
4. Invalid
5. Reproduction
6. Orchestrate
7. Sequential
8. Insignificant
9. Supple
10. Alienate

Exercise B

1. Orchestrate
2. Affirmative
3. Mentality
4. Alienate
5. Simultaneous
6. Insignificant
7. Sequential
8. Supple
9. Invalid
10. Reproduction

Exercise C

1. Affirmative
2. Reproduction
3. Mentality
4. Simultaneous
5. Alienate
6. Supple
7. Insignificant
8. Orchestrate
9. Invalid
10. Sequential

Vocabulary 6

Exercise A

1. Meagre
2. Defamation
3. Appraise
4. Loiter
5. Elude
6. Existential
7. Abstain
8. Aversion
9. Condensation
10. Treachery

Exercise B

1. Condensation
2. Loiter
3. Existential
4. Abstain
5. Treachery
6. Aversion
7. Meagre
8. Elude
9. Appraise
10. Defamation

Exercise C

1. Existential
2. Condensation
3. Appraise
4. Loiter
5. Aversion
6. Elude
7. Treachery
8. Abstain
9. Meagre
10. Defamation

Vocabulary 7

Exercise A

1. Incoherent
2. Overtone
3. Excavate
4. Innate
5. Conscience
6. Foreseeable
7. Coincide
8. Indispensable
9. Utility
10. Fretful

Exercise B

1. Fretful
2. Utility
3. Incoherent
4. Overtone
5. Innate
6. Coincide
7. Indispensable
8. Excavate
9. Conscience
10. Foreseeable

Exercise C

1. Overtone
2. Indispensable
3. Conscience
4. Excavate
5. Coincide
6. Innate
7. Fretful
8. Foreseeable
9. Incoherent
10. Utility

Answers

Vocabulary 8

Exercise A

1. Influx
2. Nuance
3. Concession
4. Correlation
5. Inert
6. Acquisition
7. Candour
8. Span
9. Bask
10. Offspring

Exercise B

1. Concession
2. Span
3. Offspring
4. Candour
5. Correlation
6. Acquisition
7. Inert
8. Nuance
9. Influx
10. Bask

Exercise C

1. Correlation
2. Acquisition
3. Bask
4. Inert
5. Concession
6. Candour
7. Span
8. Influx
9. Offspring
10. Nuance

Vocabulary 9

Exercise A

1. Commentary
2. Ephemeral
3. Mildew
4. Medieval
5. Illusory
6. Interlude
7. Parasitic
8. Provocation
9. Disconcerting
10. Patriarch

Exercise B

1. Medieval
2. Mildew
3. Illusory
4. Disconcerting
5. Patriarch
6. Commentary
7. Interlude
8. Parasitic
9. Provocation
10. Ephemeral

Exercise C

1. Parasitic
2. Patriarch
3. Provocation
4. Interlude
5. Ephemeral
6. Mildew
7. Medieval
8. Disconcerting
9. Illusory
10. Commentary

Vocabulary 10

Exercise A

1. Matinee
2. Niche
3. Upturn
4. Omniscient
5. Antiquated
6. Seethe
7. Import
8. Enclave
9. Inkling
10. Paradox

Exercise B

1. Enclave
2. Import
3. Seethe
4. Upturn
5. Matinee
6. Omniscient
7. Antiquated
8. Paradox
9. Niche
10. Inkling

Exercise C

1. Seethe
2. Antiquated
3. Matinee
4. Paradox
5. Niche
6. Import
7. Upturn
8. Inkling
9. Enclave
10. Omniscient

Vocabulary 11

Exercise A

1. Exponential
2. Tell-tale
3. Cyclical
4. Pagan
5. Viscous
6. Matriarch
7. Pragmatic
8. Irksome
9. Sprightly
10. Remiss

Exercise B

1. Remiss
2. Pragmatic
3. Pagan
4. Sprightly
5. Tell-tale
6. Exponential
7. Cyclical
8. Viscous
9. Matriarch
10. Irksome

Exercise C

1. Viscous
2. Matriarch
3. Irksome
4. Remiss
5. Pragmatic
6. Tell-tale
7. Cyclical
8. Pagan
9. Sprightly
10. Exponential

Answers

Vocabulary 12

Exercise A

1. Wintry
2. Mania
3. Eccentric
4. Crag
5. Writhe
6. Premonition
7. Lithe
8. Pious
9. Intimacy
10. Antagonise

Exercise B

1. Premonition
2. Crag
3. Mania
4. Intimacy
5. Pious
6. Eccentric
7. Writhe
8. Wintry
9. Antagonise
10. Lithe

Exercise C

1. Pious
2. Antagonise
3. Crag
4. Premonition
5. Writhe
6. Lithe
7. Intimacy
8. Mania
9. Eccentric
10. Wintry

Vocabulary 13

Exercise A

1. Bashful
2. Quip
3. Brimful
4. Suggestive
5. Reproach
6. Glacial
7. Waive
8. Buoyant
9. Genesis
10. Aflame

Exercise B

1. Genesis
2. Glacial
3. Quip
4. Waive
5. Suggestive
6. Buoyant
7. Brimful
8. Bashful
9. Reproach
10. Aflame

Exercise C

1. Buoyant
2. Suggestive
3. Waive
4. Bashful
5. Aflame
6. Genesis
7. Quip
8. Glacial
9. Brimful
10. Reproach

Vocabulary 14

Exercise A

1. Quizzical
2. Upbraid
3. Irresolute
4. Euphemism
5. Genteel
6. Calorie
7. Spiny
8. Feign
9. Uppermost
10. Berth

Exercise B

1. Spiny
2. Uppermost
3. Upbraid
4. Calorie
5. Berth
6. Quizzical
7. Euphemism
8. Feign
9. Genteel
10. Irresolute

Exercise C

1. Berth
2. Euphemism
3. Genteel
4. Quizzical
5. Spiny
6. Irresolute
7. Upbraid
8. Calorie
9. Feign
10. Uppermost

Answers

Vocabulary 15

Exercise A

1. Franchise
2. Animosity
3. Languish
4. Reprimand
5. Glib
6. Autocrat
7. Prejudice
8. Fulfilment
9. Delegate
10. Impartial

Exercise B

1. Impartial
2. Fulfilment
3. Glib
4. Autocrat
5. Prejudice
6. Delegate
7. Franchise
8. Reprimand
9. Animosity
10. Languish

Exercise C

1. Autocrat
2. Impartial
3. Languish
4. Animosity
5. Franchise
6. Glib
7. Fulfilment
8. Delegate
9. Prejudice
10. Reprimand

Vocabulary 16

Exercise A

1. Acquire
2. Deranged
3. Flatten
4. Undisturbed
5. Implication
6. Mould
7. Subordinate
8. Cram
9. Endure
10. Assassinate

Exercise B

1. Deranged
2. Flatten
3. Subordinate
4. Mould
5. Assassinate
6. Acquire
7. Cram
8. Implication
9. Undisturbed
10. Endure

Exercise C

1. Undisturbed
2. Subordinate
3. Acquire
4. Mould
5. Deranged
6. Assassinate
7. Endure
8. Flatten
9. Implication
10. Cram

Vocabulary 17

Exercise A

1. Wary
2. Bayonet
3. Particularly
4. Makeshift
5. Uncomfortable
6. Wander
7. Panic
8. Weep
9. Insurance
10. Procure

Exercise B

1. Weep
2. Procure
3. Wary
4. Insurance
5. Bayonet
6. Wander
7. Particularly
8. Makeshift
9. Uncomfortable
10. Panic

Exercise C

1. Bayonet
2. Insurance
3. Panic
4. Wary
5. Makeshift
6. Uncomfortable
7. Procure
8. Wander
9. Weep
10. Particularly

Answers

Vocabulary 18

Exercise A

1. Tender
2. Clank
3. Exaggerate
4. Decency
5. Scamper
6. Skim
7. Grimace
8. Bolt
9. Capable
10. Whirl

Exercise B

1. Capable
2. Skim
3. Grimace
4. Bolt
5. Whirl
6. Exaggerate
7. Decency
8. Clank
9. Scamper
10. Tender

Exercise C

1. Grimace
2. Decency
3. Scamper
4. Skim
5. Clank
6. Capable
7. Tender
8. Exaggerate
9. Whirl
10. Bolt

Vocabulary 19

Exercise A

1. Infrastructure
2. Cower
3. Squadron
4. Stammer
5. Triumphantly
6. Flurry
7. Blueprint
8. Mountainous
9. Gesture
10. Senseless

Exercise B

1. Stammer
2. Triumphantly
3. Gesture
4. Infrastructure
5. Squadron
6. Cower
7. Mountainous
8. Flurry
9. Senseless
10. Blueprint

Exercise C

1. Senseless
2. Gesture
3. Triumphantly
4. Infrastructure
5. Cower
6. Blueprint
7. Flurry
8. Stammer
9. Mountainous
10. Squadron

Vocabulary 20

Exercise A

1. Ravenous
2. Leaden
3. Incendiary
4. Beloved
5. Singular
6. Buckle
7. Credentials
8. Mournfully
9. Plateau
10. Harried

Exercise B

1. Mournfully
2. Harried
3. Incendiary
4. Buckle
5. Ravenous
6. Singular
7. Leaden
8. Beloved
9. Credentials
10. Plateau

Exercise C

1. Credentials
2. Singular
3. Ravenous
4. Mournfully
5. Plateau
6. Buckle
7. Beloved
8. Leaden
9. Incendiary
10. Harried